Farm Girl Quilts

Celebrating the Country Life

Tammy Johnson and Avis Shirer

Martingale®
& C O M P A N Y

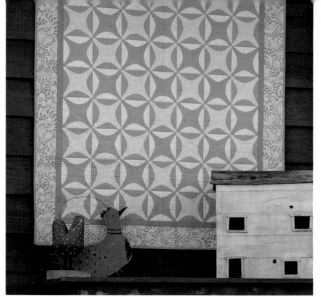

Farm Girl Quilts: Celebrating the Country Life
© 2011 by Tammy Johnson and Avis Shirer

That Patchwork Place® is an
imprint of Martingale & Company®.

Martingale & Company
19021 120th Ave. NE, Suite 102
Bothell, WA 98011-9511
www.martingale-pub.com

Printed in China
16 15 14 13 12 11   8 7 6 5 4 3 2 1

Library of Congress Cataloging-in-Publication Data
is available upon request.

ISBN: 978-1-60468-061-4

Mission Statement

*Dedicated to providing quality products
and service to inspire creativity.*

Credits

President & CEO: Tom Wierzbicki
Editor in Chief: Mary V. Green
Managing Editor: Tina Cook
Developmental Editor: Karen Costello Soltys
Technical Editor: Ellen Pahl
Copy Editor: Marcy Heffernan
Design Director: Stan Green
Production Manager: Regina Girard
Illustrator: Laurel Strand
Cover & Text Designer: Regina Girard
Photographer: Brent Kane

Special thanks to Rosemary and Cliff Bailey
of Snohomish, Washington, for generously
allowing us to photograph at their farm.

Contents

Introduction

Farm life is very special to us. We were both born and raised on farms. Our families have been involved in farming for generations, going back to our great-great-grandparents. They all knew that farming was special—making a living off the earth, tending to the crops, and then harvesting a bountiful crop. It meant hard work, but it was rewarding. We are extremely proud of our heritage and are delighted to give you a glimpse through our quilts of what farm life is like.

We hope you enjoy the quilt projects presented in this book. Here's to finding your place on the farm!

Tammy and Avis
The Hip Chick Farm Girls

Quiltmaking Basics

The techniques we use to make our quilts include basic rotary cutting, some shortcut piecing, and fusible appliqué. We like to finish the appliqué with machine blanket stitching for a decorative touch. You may be familiar with all of these techniques already, but if you need some guidance, we've covered the basics for you in this section.

Supplies

You'll need just a few essentials to make the quilts in this book.

Rotary-cutting tools: You'll need a cutting mat, a rotary cutter, and clear acrylic rulers. Rulers come in many shapes and sizes. A 6" x 24" ruler and a 12½" square ruler are good sizes to start with.

Sewing machine: A sewing machine in good working order is a must-have. The majority of stitching is done with a straight stitch. We use the machine blanket stitch to finish the edges of fused appliqués. If you plan to machine quilt your projects as we've done, you'll find a walking foot and a darning foot very helpful.

Fusible web: If you want to stitch around the edges of the fused appliqués, make sure to use a lightweight fusible web.

Batting: While there are many types of batting available, we used cotton batting for all of the quilts in this book. Cotton batting gives a very flat look, and if the finished quilt is washed, it will take on the crinkled look of an antique quilt.

Rotary Cutting

Rotary cutting will make the process of constructing a quilt much more accurate and much faster than if you cut the pieces with scissors. The following steps will guide you in the process.

1. Fold the fabric with the selvages together. Lay the fabric on the cutting mat with the fold toward you, aligning the fabric with a horizontal line on the mat.

2. Lay a small square ruler along the folded edge of the fabric, aligning the ruler with the folded edge of the fabric. Then lay a long ruler to the left of the square ruler so that the edges touch.

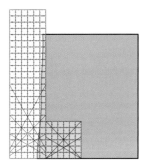

3. Remove the square ruler, keeping the long ruler in place. Cut along the right edge of the long ruler with a rotary cutter. The edge of the fabric is now straight and ready for you to cut strips.

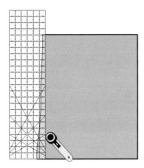

4. Line up the straight edge of the fabric with the line on the ruler that corresponds to the required measurement. Cut the strip.

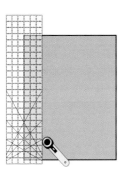

5. To crosscut the strips, trim the selvages off the ends of the strip. Line up the left side of the strip with the correct ruler line. Cut along the right edge of the ruler.

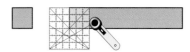

6. To cut a half-square triangle, cut a square the size indicated in the cutting instructions. Lay a ruler across the square diagonally and cut from corner to corner. One square will yield two half-square triangles.

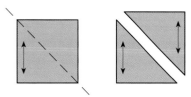

7. To cut a quarter-square triangle, cut a square the size indicated in the cutting instructions. Lay a ruler across the square diagonally and cut from corner to corner. Without moving the fabric, lay the ruler in the opposite direction from corner to corner and cut. One square will yield four quarter-square triangles.

Folded Corners

One piecing shortcut we often use when making blocks is the folded-corner technique. It makes quick work of adding diagonal corners to squares and rectangles and gives neat and accurate results. The block instructions will give the sizes to cut. The following steps explain how to do the piecing.

1. Fold the square that will be used to make the corner in half diagonally and crease it to mark the stitching line. Or, use a pencil and ruler to draw a diagonal line from corner to corner on the wrong side of the square.

Crease or pencil line

2. Place the square right sides together with the strip, rectangle, or larger square as shown in the project illustration. Make sure the diagonal line is angled in the correct direction, and then stitch on the creased or drawn stitching line.

Stitch.

3. Trim away the outer corner of the square, cutting ¼" from the stitching line. Leave the bottom layer (square, rectangle, or strip) intact. This will help stabilize the corner. Flip open the top square of fabric and press to complete the folded corner.

Trim.   Press.

Fusible Appliqué

For this technique, the templates need to be reversed from the image shown in the completed quilt. In this book, we've already reversed the patterns for you.

1. Trace the pattern from the book onto the paper side of the fusible-web material. You may want to make a template from cardstock or template plastic if you'll be tracing the pattern many times.

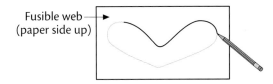

2. Cut out the shape, cutting about ¼" *outside* of the traced line. Do not cut on the line!

3. Place the fusible-web shape, traced side up, on the wrong side of the appropriate fabric. Use your iron to press the fusible web onto the fabric, following the manufacturer's instructions. Cut out the shape along the traced line. Remove the paper backing.

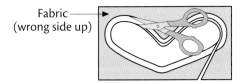

4. Place the template with the shiny adhesive side down on the right side of the background fabric and press in place. When appliquéing several shapes to a block, we suggest that you position all of the shapes before fusing anything in place. This allows for placement adjustment if needed.

5. Finish the edges of the appliqués by stitching around them with a decorative stitch and matching or coordinating thread. We used a machine blanket stitch for the appliqués in this book.

Adding Borders

It's always a good idea to measure the center of your quilt before cutting and adding borders. Measure through the center of the quilt because the edges may have stretched slightly during construction.

1. Measure the length of the quilt top through the center. Cut the side border strips to this length, piecing as needed. Pin and sew the borders to the sides of the quilt, matching the centers and ends. Press the seam allowances toward the border strips.

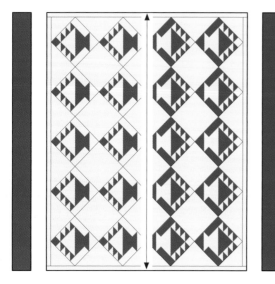

2. Measure the width of the quilt top through the center, including the borders just added. Cut the top and bottom borders to this length, piecing as needed. Pin and sew the borders to the top and bottom of the quilt, matching the centers

and ends. Press the seam allowances toward the border strips.

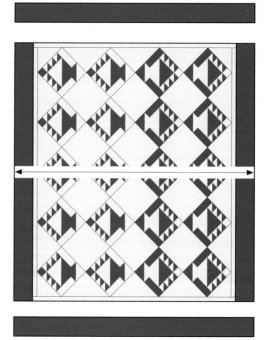

Quilting

When the quilt top is done, make a "sandwich" by layering the backing fabric, batting, and quilt top. The batting and backing pieces should be approximately 6" larger than the quilt top.

1. Lay the backing fabric right side down on a flat surface. Secure the edges with masking tape to keep the backing smooth but not stretched.

2. Lay the batting piece on top of the backing. Smooth out all the wrinkles, and then center the quilt top right side up over the batting.

3. Baste the sandwich using a needle and thread, safety pins, or basting spray.

4. Quilt as desired by hand or machine. The quilts in this book were machine quilted.

Binding

We like to use single-fold binding to finish the quilt edges. For this, we cut binding strips 1½" wide. If you prefer a double-fold binding, we've allowed enough fabric in the materials lists to cut strips up to 2½" wide.

1. Cut 1½"-wide strips across the width of the fabric as directed in the project instructions. Join the strips using a diagonal seam to make one strip long enough to go all the way around the quilt plus at least 10" for joining strips, turning the corners, and finishing the ends.

2. Begin at the middle of the bottom edge of the quilt and align the raw edge of the binding with the raw edge of the quilt top, right sides together. Start stitching 1" from the end of the binding strip through all the layers using a ¼" seam allowance. Stop stitching ¼" from the corner of the quilt. Backstitch and cut the thread. Turn the quilt so you can sew down the next side. Fold the binding strip up, so the fold forms a 45° angle. Bring the binding strip down onto itself. Stitch along the edge, again using a ¼" seam allowance.

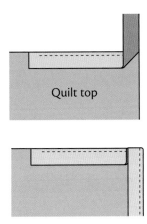

3. Repeat this process for each corner. When you're close to the beginning of the binding, fold back the 1" tail that was left at the start of the binding. Then overlap the other end of the binding with the 1" folded edge, and continue stitching to hold all three layers in place. Trim away any excess binding.

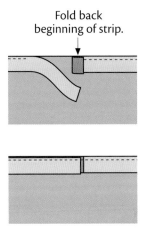

Fold back beginning of strip.

4. Using a long ruler and rotary cutter, trim the batting and backing even with the edge of the quilt top. Fold the binding over the raw edge of the quilt. Hand stitch the binding in place using a blind stitch, turning under ¼" on the raw edge of the binding strip as you go.

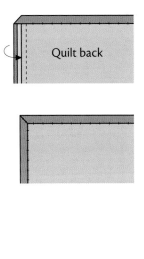

Quilt back

Grandpa's Weathervane

Materials

Yardage is based on 42"-wide fabric.

⅓ yard *each* of 8 assorted tan prints, plaids, and striped fabrics for House blocks and spacer squares

¾ yard of black-and-brown mottled print for weathervane appliqué, roof appliqués on two houses, and binding

⅝ yard of brown checked fabric for outer border

¼ yard *each* of 2 light prints for House block backgrounds

¼ yard or 8" square of red print for center weathervane appliqué with 8 points

¼ yard or 8" square of red mini-checked fabric for center weathervane appliqué with 4 points

¼ yard of red print for inner border

⅛ yard *each* of 2 black prints for house-roof appliqués

⅛ yard or 4" x 8" piece *each* of 2 light tan prints for front-room appliqués

⅛ yard of brown striped fabric for window-frame and porch-post appliqués on 2 houses

⅛ yard of cream fabric for window-frame and porch-post appliqués on 2 houses

⅛ yard of gold print for window appliqués

⅛ yard of gray print for window appliqués

Scraps (2" x 11" pieces) of 4 green fabrics for ground

Scraps (2" x 14" pieces) of 3 red fabrics for chimneys and doors

Scrap (4" x 4" piece) of gold fabric for center-circle appliqué on weathervane

2½ yards of fabric for backing

44" x 54" piece of batting

1¼ yards of 18"-wide fusible web

Cutting

From the assorted tan fabrics, choose 2 for each house: 1 for the wide logs and 1 for the narrow logs. The appliqué patterns are on pages 16–19. For more information on cutting pieces for fusible appliqué, refer to "Fusible Appliqué" on page 17.

From *each* of 4 assorted tan fabrics for the wide logs, cut:

5 rectangles, 1½" x 8½"

2 rectangles, 1½" x 5½"

2 rectangles, 1½" x 2½"

3 squares, 5½" x 5½"

From *each* of 4 assorted tan fabrics for the narrow logs, cut:

4 rectangles, 1" x 8½"

2 rectangles, 1" x 5½"

2 rectangles, 1" x 2½"

3 squares, 5½" x 5½"

From *each* of the 2 light background prints, cut:
4 rectangles, 2½" x 3½"
6 squares, 2½" x 2½"
4 rectangles, 1½" x 12½"
4 squares, 1½" x 1½"

From *each* of the 2 black prints, cut:
1 rectangle, 2½" x 8½"
1 porch-roof appliqué
1 front-room roof appliqué

From the black-and-brown mottled print, cut:
5 binding strips, 1½" x 42"
2 rectangles, 2½" x 8½"
2 porch-roof appliqués
2 front-room roof appliqués
1 large weathervane-circle appliqué
2 long arrow appliqués
2 short arrow appliqués
N, S, E, and W appliqués

From *each* of the 4 green fabrics, cut:
1 rectangle, 1½" x 10½"

From *each* of 2 of the red scraps, cut:
2 rectangles, 1½" x 3½"

From the remaining red scrap, cut:
8 squares, 1½" x 1½"

From *each* of the 2 light tan prints, cut:
2 front room appliqués

From the gold print, cut:
8 window appliqués

From the gray print, cut:
8 window appliqués

From the brown striped fabric, cut:
8 window-frame appliqués
4 porch-post appliqués

From the cream fabric, cut:
8 window frame appliqués
4 porch post appliqués

From the red print, cut:
1 weathervane-center appliqué with 8 points

From the red mini-checked fabric, cut:
1 weathervane-center appliqué with 4 points

From the gold fabric scrap, cut:
1 weathervane center-circle appliqué

From the red print for inner border, cut:
2 strips, 1½" x 40½"
2 strips, 1½" x 32½"

From the brown checked fabric, cut:
2 strips, 3½" x 42½"
2 strips, 3½" x 38½"

House Block Construction

1. Sew five tan 1½" x 8½" rectangles and four tan 1" x 8½" rectangles together, alternating them as shown. Make four.

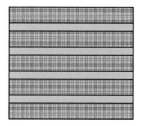

Make 4.

2. Sew two tan 1" x 2½" rectangles and two tan 1½" x 2½" rectangles together, keeping the same two tan prints together as in step 1. Sew two tan 1" x 5½" and two tan 1½" x 5½" rectangles together. Make four of each.

Make 4 of each.

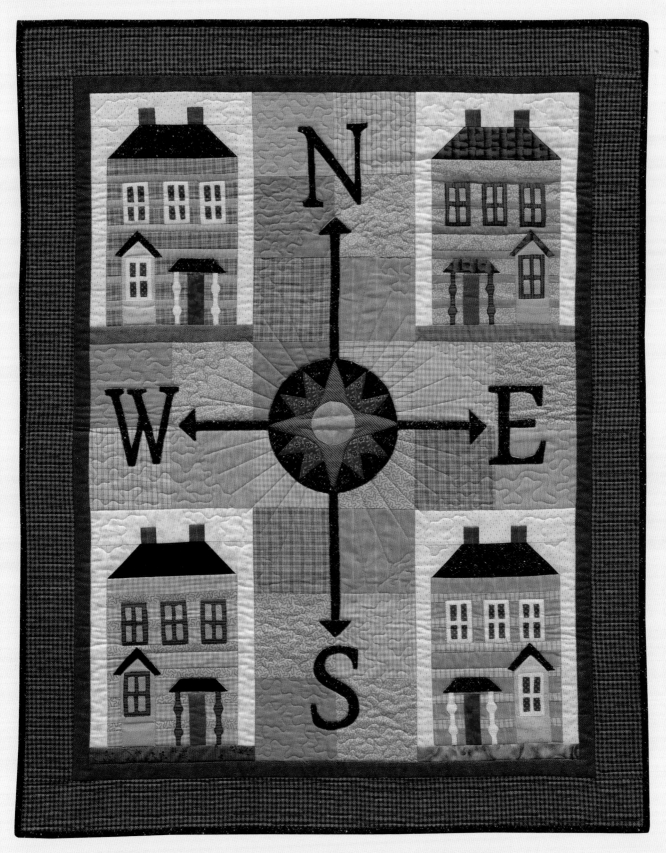

Quilted by Sue Urich • **Finished quilt:** 38½" x 48½" • **Finished block:** 10" x 15"

3. Sew the units from step 2 to a red 1½" x 3½" rectangle as shown. Note that the 5½"-wide units will be on the left side of two blocks and on the right side of two blocks.

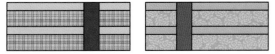

Make 2 of each.

4. Add the matching unit from step 1 to the top of each unit from step 3. Make two of each.

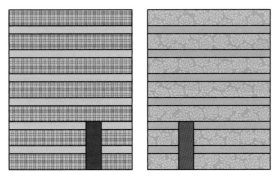

Make 2 of each.

5. For the roof unit, refer to "Folded Corners" on page 6 to mark and lay a light 2½" square on top of a black 2½" x 8½" rectangle. Stitch diagonally across the light square, trim, and press. Repeat with a second light 2½" square on the opposite end.

6. Sew the roof unit to the top of a house unit. Add the two light 1½" x 12½" rectangles to the sides and the green 1½" x 10½" rectangle to the bottom.

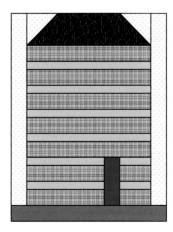

7. To make the chimney unit, sew a red 1½" square and a light 1½" square together. Make two. Sew these units, two light 2½" x 3½" rectangles, and one light 2½" square together as shown.

8. Add the chimney unit to the top of a house unit.

9. Repeat steps 5–8 to make four blocks.

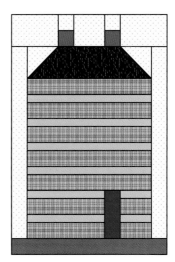

House Appliqués

Refer to "Fusible Appliqué" on page 7 and to the photo on page 13 for placement guidance. You'll need four windows, four window frames, one front room, one front-room roof, one porch roof, and two porch posts for each house block.

1. Position the front-room appliqué on the block. Place it on the right side of two blocks and on the left side of two blocks. Position a front-room roof on the front room.

2. Position four windows and add a window frame on top of each window.

3. Position two porch posts and one porch roof.

4. When you're happy with the placement, fuse in place.

Quilt Assembly

1. Stitch six tan 5½" squares together as shown. Sew a house block to each side so that the front room is on the outer side of each section. Make two sections.

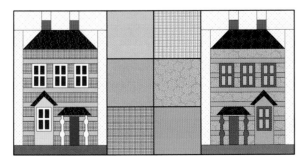

Make 2.

2. Stitch together the remaining 12 tan 5½" squares in two rows of six squares each.

3. Sew the rows of squares and the House block sections together as shown.

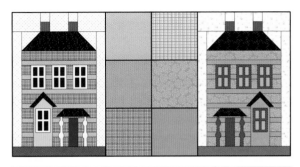

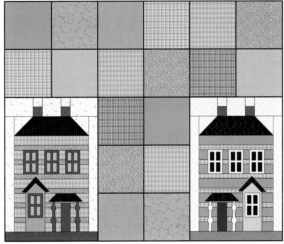

Weathervane Appliqué

1. Prepare the large center circle, the center shape with eight points, the center shape with four points, the small center circle, two long arrows, two short arrows, and the letters N, S, E, and W.

2. Position the large center circle first. Then position the long arrows above and below the circle, centering the arrows on the seam line. Position the short arrows to the left and right of the circle, again, centering them on the seam line. Tuck the ends under the center circle.

3. Position the center-circle shapes and the small center circle.

4. Position the letters.

5. When you're happy with the placement, fuse in place.

Borders and Finishing

It's always a good idea to measure the length and width of your quilt through the center before cutting borders. See "Adding Borders" on page 8. If your dimensions vary from those given, cut the borders to match your quilt.

1. Stitch the two red 1½" x 40½" strips to the sides of the quilt. Then sew the two red 1½" x 32½" strips to the top and bottom.

2. For the outer border, sew the two brown 3½" x 42½" strips to the sides of the quilt. Sew the two brown 3½" x 38½" strips to the top and bottom.

3. Layer the quilt top, batting, and backing. Quilt as desired.

4. Sew the five black-and-brown mottled print 1½"-wide binding strips together, end to end. Sew the binding to the quilt top, referring to page 9 for more binding help.

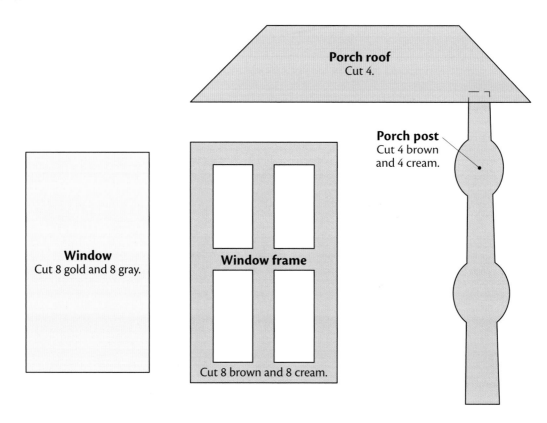

Porch roof
Cut 4.

Porch post
Cut 4 brown and 4 cream.

Window
Cut 8 gold and 8 gray.

Window frame
Cut 8 brown and 8 cream.

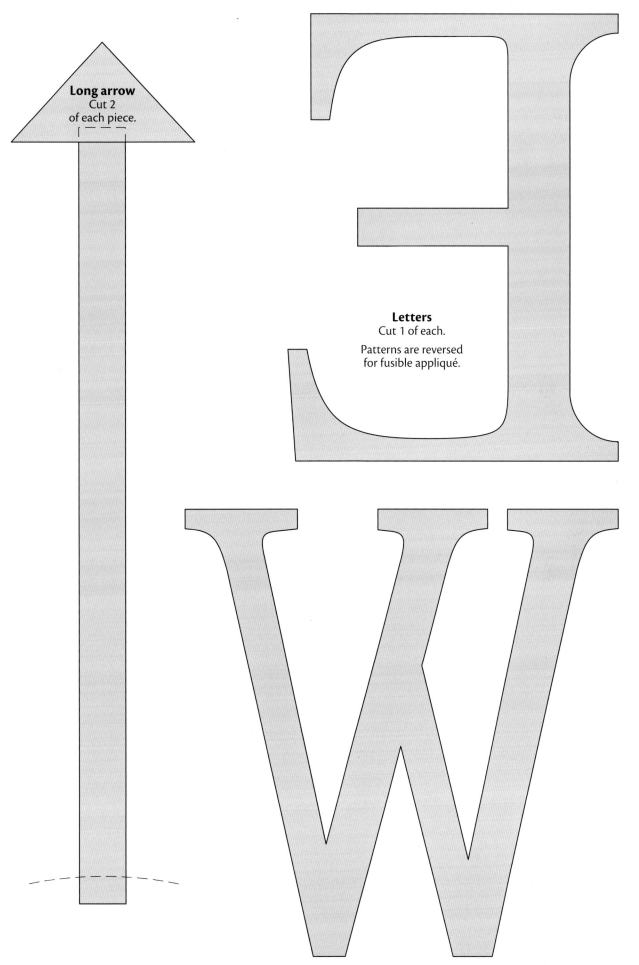

Long arrow
Cut 2
of each piece.

Letters
Cut 1 of each.

Patterns are reversed
for fusible appliqué.

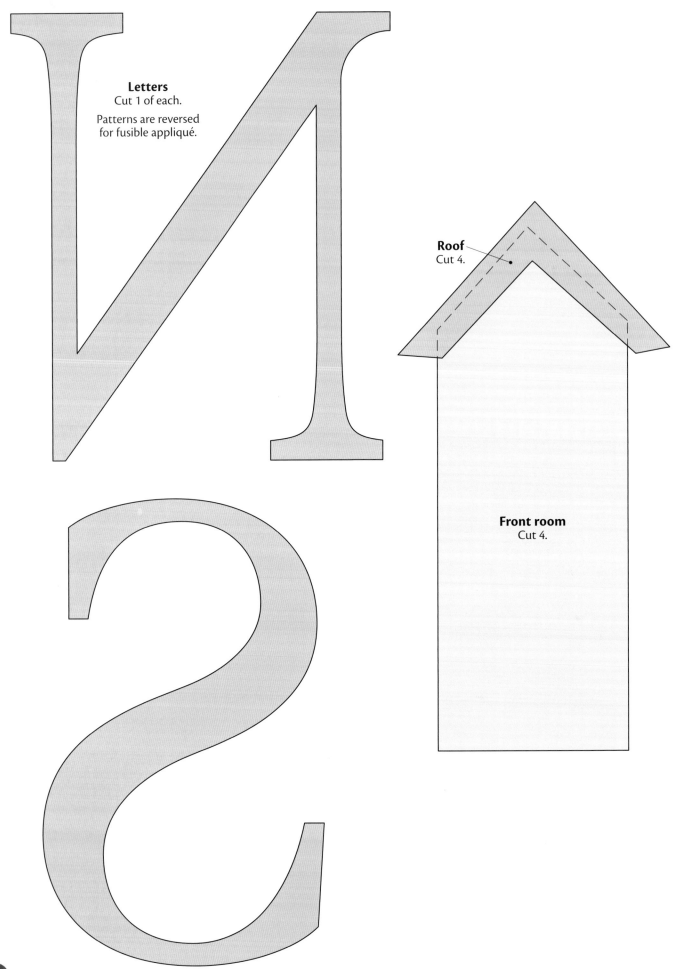

Letters
Cut 1 of each.

Patterns are reversed
for fusible appliqué.

Roof
Cut 4.

Front room
Cut 4.

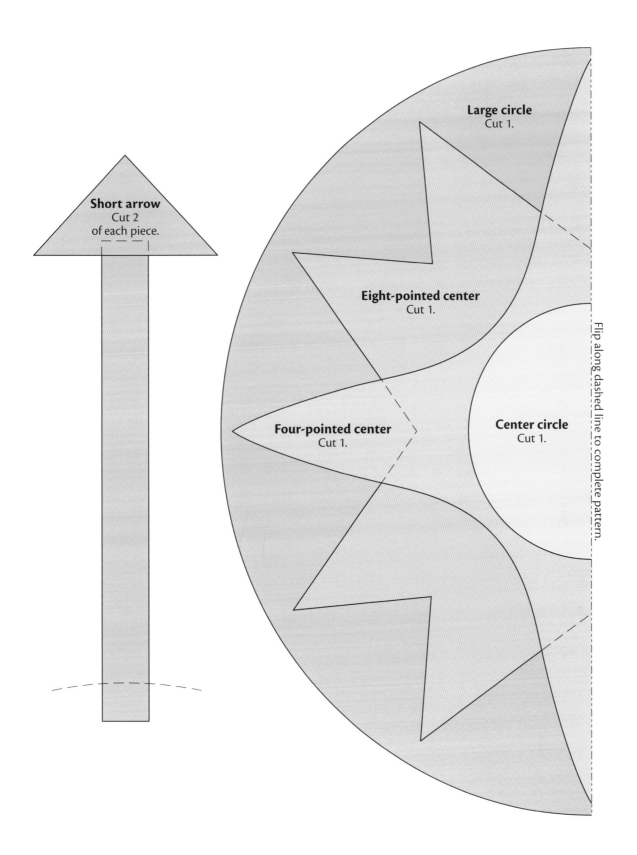

Short arrow
Cut 2
of each piece.

Large circle
Cut 1.

Eight-pointed center
Cut 1.

Four-pointed center
Cut 1.

Center circle
Cut 1.

Flip along dashed line to complete pattern.

Blue Harvestore Baskets

I f you're a true Midwestern farm girl, you know what a Harvestore is. I've always thought those blue Harvestore silos were a thing of beauty; they're a brilliant royal blue and across the top, in bold, white letters is the name Harvestore. For all of our non-farm girl-friends, a Harvestore is a large silo that holds silage. What's silage? It's a ground-up mixture of corn (including the stalk, leaves, and ears of immature corn) that's fed to cows, and it needs to be kept clean and dry to offer good nutrition. A blue Harvestore was the ideal way to keep it clean and dry. Unfortunately, very few farmers around us raise cattle anymore, so the blue Harvestore silos stand empty as do the cattle sheds that once housed the cattle. The colors in this quilt duplicate my love affair with those massive blue silos, and the quilt is a gentle reminder of my farming roots.

~Avis

Materials

Yardage is based on 42"-wide fabric.

3½ yards of white-and-blue print for Basket blocks, setting blocks, setting triangles, and inner border

2⅝ yards of blue fabric for the Basket blocks, outer border, and binding

3⅝ yards of fabric for backing

63" x 76" piece of batting

Cutting

Half of the blocks in this quilt have baskets that are blue with a white background and half of the blocks have baskets that are white with a blue background. It's easier to keep all the pieces straight if you cut and sew the blocks in two batches, by color. We've written the instructions for constructing blocks with blue baskets and white background first.

Blue Basket Blocks

From the blue fabric, cut:

1 strip, 6⅛" x 42", crosscut into 5 squares, 6⅛" x 6⅛"; cut each square in half diagonally to yield 10 triangles

3 strips, 2⅝" x 42", crosscut into 40 squares, 2⅝" x 2⅝"; cut each square in half diagonally to yield 80 triangles

1 strip, 2¼" x 42", crosscut into 10 squares, 2¼" x 2¼"

From the white-and-blue print, cut:

1 strip, 6⅛" x 42", crosscut into 5 squares, 6⅛" x 6⅛"; cut each square in half diagonally to yield 10 triangles

1 strip, 4⅜" x 42", crosscut into 5 squares, 4⅜" x 4⅜"; cut each square in half diagonally to yield 10 triangles

2 strips, 2⅝" x 42", crosscut into 30 squares, 2⅝" x 2⅝"; cut each square in half diagonally to yield 60 triangles

4 strips, 2¼" x 42", crosscut into 20 rectangles, 2¼" x 5¾"

White Basket Blocks

From the white-and-blue print, cut:

1 strip, 6⅛" x 42", crosscut into 5 squares, 6⅛" x 6⅛"; cut each square in half diagonally to yield 10 triangles

3 strips, 2⅝" x 42", crosscut into 40 squares, 2⅝" x 2⅝"; cut each square in half diagonally to yield 80 triangles

1 strip, 2¼" x 42", crosscut into 10 squares, 2¼" x 2¼"

From the blue fabric, cut:

1 strip, 6⅛" x 42", crosscut into 5 squares, 6⅛" x 6⅛"; cut each square in half diagonally to yield 10 triangles

1 strip, 4⅜" x 42", crosscut into 5 squares, 4⅜" x 4⅜"; cut each square in half diagonally to yield 10 triangles

2 strips, 2⅝" x 42", crosscut into 30 squares, 2⅝" x 2⅝"; cut each square in half diagonally to yield 60 triangles

4 strips, 2¼" x 42", crosscut into 20 rectangles, 2¼" x 5¾"

Setting Squares, Triangles, Borders, and Binding

From the white-and-blue print, cut:

3 strips, 9¼" x 42", crosscut into 12 squares, 9¼" x 9¼"

2 strips, 13⅝" x 42", crosscut into 4 squares, 13⅝" x 13⅝"; cut each square into quarters diagonally to yield 16 triangles (2 are extra)

2 squares, 7⅛" x 7⅛", cut each square in half diagonally to yield 4 triangles

6 strips, 1½" x 42"

From the blue fabric, cut:

7 strips, 3½" x 42"

7 binding strips, 1½" x 42"

Blue Basket Block Construction

1. Stitch together a blue 6⅛" triangle and a white 6⅛" triangle.

2. Sew a blue 2⅝" triangle and a white 2⅝" triangle together. Make six units. Sew these units together into two rows of three blocks each as shown.

3. Sew one row from step 2 to the top of the unit from step 1. Sew a blue 2¼" square to the remaining row as shown, and sew this row to the left side of the unit.

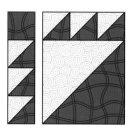

4. Sew a blue 2⅝" triangle to a white rectangle. Make two units as shown. Sew these to the unit from step 3.

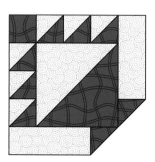

Quilted by Sue Urich • **Finished quilt:** 58" x 70½" • **Finished block:** 8¾" x 8¾"

5. Add the white 4⅜" triangle as shown to complete the block. Repeat to make 10 blocks.

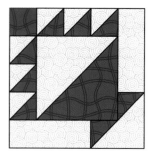

Make 10.

White Basket Block Construction

Follow steps 1–5 for the blue Basket block beginning on page 22, replacing each white piece with a blue piece and each blue piece with a white piece. Make 10 blocks.

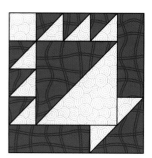

Make 10.

Quilt Assembly

Sew the blocks, setting squares, setting triangles, and corner triangles together in diagonal rows as shown. Pay close attention to block placement.

Borders and Finishing

1. For the inner border, sew the six white 1½" x 42" strips together end to end.

2. Refer to "Adding Borders" on page 8 to measure the quilt, cut, and add the inner borders to the sides, and then the top and bottom of the quilt.

3. Sew the seven blue 3½" x 42" strips together end to end and repeat step 2 to add the outer border.

4. Layer the quilt top, batting, and backing. Quilt as desired.

5. Bind the quilt using the blue 1½" x 42" strips. Refer to "Binding" on page 9 for more information.

Mrs. Nodland's Chicken Farm

Mrs. Nodland lived just down the road from the farm I grew up on. She and her husband had two huge chicken houses where they raised laying chickens and sold eggs straight off the farm. She was quite a lady—always ready for a lively conversation as she sorted the eggs. Most of her hens laid white eggs, but she also had some that laid brown eggs. I always thought the brown eggs were the prettiest eggs I'd ever seen—much too pretty to crack and eat! The colors in this quilt and the gentle rounded shapes remind me of those wonderful, farm-fresh eggs and all the nice chats we had with Mrs. Nodland.

~Tammy

Materials

Yardage is based on 42"-wide fabric.
1¾ yards of cream print for blocks and appliqués
1¾ yards of taupe solid for blocks and appliqués
⅔ yard of tan-and-taupe print for outer border
⅓ yard of taupe-and-cream print for inner border
½ yard of tan-and-taupe print for binding
3 yards of fabric for backing
50" x 60" piece of batting
4 yards of 18"-wide fusible web

Cutting

The appliqué pattern is on page 29. For more information on cutting pieces for fusible appliqué, refer to "Fusible Appliqué" on page 7.

From the cream print, cut:
5 strips, 5½" x 42", crosscut into 31 squares, 5½" x 5½"
32 appliqué shapes

From the taupe solid, cut:
5 strips, 5½" x 42", crosscut into 32 squares, 5½" x 5½"
31 appliqué shapes

From the taupe-and-cream print, cut:
5 strips, 1½" x 42"

From the tan-and-taupe outer border fabric, cut:
5 strips, 4" x 42"

From the tan-and-taupe binding fabric, cut:
6 strips, 1½" x 42"

Block Appliqué

Refer to "Fusible Appliqué" on page 7 as needed. You should have 32 appliqué shapes using the cream print and 31 appliqué shapes using the taupe solid.

1. Lay a cream appliqué shape on top of a taupe solid 5½" square. Align the corners of the appliqué shape with the corners of the background square. Fuse in place and stitch around the shape with a machine blanket stitch. Make 32 blocks.

2. Repeat step 1 to appliqué a taupe solid appliqué shape to a cream 5½" square. Make 31 blocks.

Make 32.   Make 31.

Quilt Assembly

Sew the blocks together in nine rows of seven blocks each, alternating the blocks as shown.

Borders and Finishing

It's always a good idea to measure the length and width of your quilt through the center before cutting borders. See "Adding Borders" on page 8. If your dimensions vary from those given, cut the borders to match your quilt.

1. For the inner border, cut two 35½"-long strips from two of the taupe-and-cream print strips. Sew the strips to the top and bottom of the quilt. Sew the remaining three 1½"-wide strips together end to end and cut two 47½"-long strips. Sew the strips to the sides of the quilt.

2. For the outer border, cut two 37½"-long strips from two of the tan-and-taupe print strips. Sew the strips to the top and bottom of the quilt. Sew the remaining three 4"-wide strips together end to end, and then cut two 54½"-long strips and sew them to the sides of the quilt.

3. Layer the quilt top, batting, and backing. Quilt as desired.

4. Sew the five tan-and-taupe 1½"-wide binding strips together end to end and sew the strips to the quilt. Refer to page 9 for more help with binding.

Quilted by Sue Urich • **Finished quilt:** 44½" x 54½" • **Finished block:** 5" x 5"

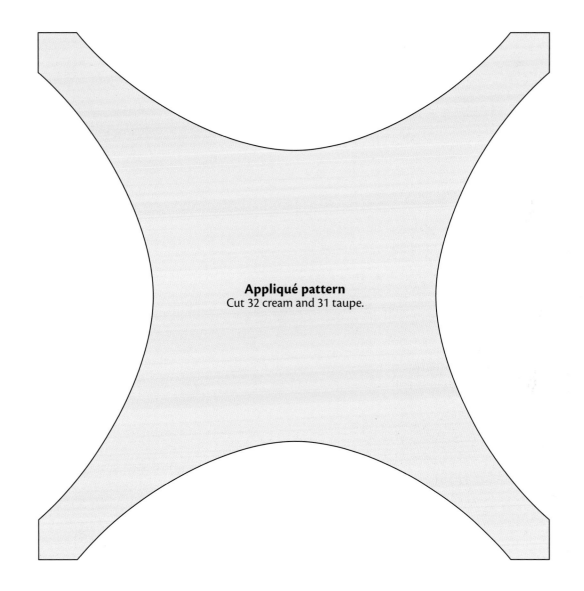

Appliqué pattern
Cut 32 cream and 31 taupe.

Fields of Red Clover

One of the pure pleasures of living in the country is the smell of freshly mown hay. We grow two varieties of hay: yellow-blossom sweet clover and sweet red clover. The main difference between these two clovers, of course, is the color of the flowers; one is yellow and the other has a pink- to rose-colored blossom. We cut the clover, rake it, let it air dry, and finally, bale it. Once the clover has gone through this process, it's fed to the cows. They *love* it!

The colors in this quilt remind me of red clover; the pink- to rose-toned fabrics look much like the blossom on the clover plant and, of course, green is for the lush stem and leaves. Now, if only this quilt could smell like clover . . . that wonderful, warm, musky scent. Close your eyes and just imagine; isn't life in the country grand?

~Avis

Materials

Yardage is based on 42"-wide fabric.

1¼ yards of dark rose print for blocks, cornerstones, outer border, and binding

¾ yard of rose solid for blocks, sashing, and inner border

½ yard of light mottled print for blocks

½ yard of light print for blocks

½ yard of light green print for blocks

¼ yard of dark green print or solid for blocks

2½ yards of fabric for backing*

45" x 56" piece of batting

*If your fabric is wide enough, you may get by with 1⅔ yards.

Cutting

From the dark rose print, cut:

4 strips, 1½" x 42", crosscut into 96 squares, 1½" x 1½"

1 strip, 2½" x 42", crosscut into 6 squares, 2½" x 2½"

4 strips, 3½" x 42"

5 binding strips, 1½" x 42"

From the rose solid, cut:

4 strips, 1½" x 42", crosscut into 96 squares, 1½" x 1½"

5 strips, 2½" x 42", crosscut into 17 rectangles, 2½" x 9½"

4 strips, 1½" x 42½"*

From the light print, cut:

6 strips, 2⅜" x 42", crosscut into 96 squares, 2⅜" x 2⅜"; cut each square in half diagonally to yield 192 triangles

From the light mottled solid, cut:

3 strips, 3⅞" x 42", crosscut into 24 squares, 3⅞" x 3⅞"; cut each square in half diagonally to yield 48 triangles

From the light green print, cut:

3 strips, 3⅞" x 42", crosscut into 24 squares, 3⅞" x 3⅞; cut each square in half diagonally to yield 48 triangles

From the dark green print, cut:

1 strip, 3½" x 42", crosscut into 12 squares, 3½" x 3½"

*Cut an extra strip if your fabric isn't 42½" wide after removing selvages.

Block Construction

1. Sew together two dark rose print 1½" squares and two rose solid 1½" squares to make a four-patch unit. Make 48.

Make 48.

2. Sew a light print triangle to each side of the four-patch unit as shown. Repeat with all 48 units.

Make 48.

3. Stitch together a light mottled solid triangle and a light green print triangle. Make 48.

Make 48.

4. Sew together four units each from steps 2 and 3 and the green 3½" square as shown. Make 12 blocks.

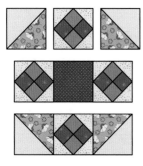 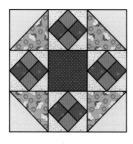

Make 12.

Quilt Assembly

1. Stitch together three blocks and two rose solid 2½" x 9½" sashing pieces. Make four rows.

Make 4.

2. Stitch together three rose solid 2½" x 9½" sashing rectangles and two dark rose print 2½" squares. Make three rows.

Make 3.

3. Stitch the block rows and sashing rows together as shown.

Quilted by Sue Urich • **Finished quilt:** 39½" x 50½" • **Finished block:** 9" x 9"

Borders and Finishing

Before cutting and adding borders, measure your quilt through the center, referring to "Adding Borders" on page 8. Cut the borders to your specific lengths if the measurements are different from those given below.

1. Sew two rose solid 1½" x 42½" strips to the sides of the quilt. You may need to piece the strips together if your fabric isn't 42½" wide. Cut two 33½"-long strips from the remaining rose solid strips and sew them to the top and bottom of the quilt.

2. For the outer border, stitch the dark rose 3½"-wide strips together end to end. Cut two 44½"-long strips and sew them to the sides of the quilt. Then cut two 39½"-long strips and sew them to the top and bottom.

3. Layer the quilt top, batting, and backing. Quilt as desired.

4. Bind using the dark rose 1½"-wide strips. Refer to page 9 for more help with binding.

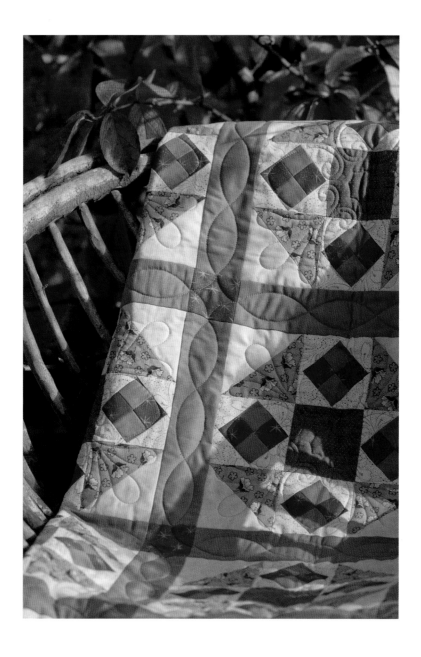

Summer Picnic Quilt

When I was young, several weeks every summer were spent walking beans. For those of you who haven't known the joy of walking beans, that's when you walk through the soybean fields pulling or chopping the weeds with a hoe. Mom and Dad and we three girls would get up early, pack a lunch, and head to the bean field for the day. It was usually very hot and very tiring, especially for our little legs. Sometimes, as a wonderful reward for our hard work, we would quit in the afternoon and go to the drive-in to pick up some fried chicken. Then we'd head to the lake for a swim to cool off and have a picnic.

As I grew older, I continued walking beans with a group of friends. Neighboring farmers hired us, and we were actually paid money! That was good, but jumping in the cool lake and having picnics in the park were worth more by far, in treasured memories.

~Tammy

Materials

Yardage is based on 42"-wide fabric.

1⅜ yards of blue checked fabric for setting squares and setting triangles

1⅜ yards of blue tone-on-tone print for outer border and binding

1 yard of cream print for blocks, star appliqués, and inner border

⅞ yard of red tone-on-tone print for blocks

⅔ yard of navy tone-on-tone print for blocks and border corner squares

3¾ yards of fabric for backing

67" x 67" piece of batting

⅝ yard of 18"-wide fusible web

Cutting

The appliqué pattern is on page 39. For more information on cutting pieces for fusible appliqué, refer to "Fusible Appliqué" on page 7.

From the navy tone-on-tone print, cut:

2 strips, 6½" x 42", crosscut into:
  9 squares, 6½" x 6½"
  4 squares, 4½" x 4½"

4 strips, 1½" x 42", crosscut into 108 squares, 1½" x 1½"

From the red tone-on-tone print, cut:

15 strips, 1½" x 42", crosscut into:
  36 rectangles, 1½" x 6½"
  36 rectangles, 1½" x 10½"

From the cream print, cut:

9 strips, 1½" x 42", crosscut into 36 rectangles, 1½" x 8½"

6 strips, 1½" x 42"

36 star appliqués

From the blue checked fabric, cut:

2 squares, 18½" x 18½", cut into quarters diagonally to yield 8 triangles

4 squares, 12½" x 12½"

2 squares, 9½" x 9½", cut in half diagonally to yield 4 triangles

From the blue tone-on-tone print, cut:

6 strips, 4½" x 42"

7 binding strips, 1½" x 42"

Block Construction

1. Sew red 1½" x 6½" rectangles to the top and bottom of a navy 6½" square.

2. Sew a navy 1½" square to each end of a red 1½" x 6½" rectangle. Make two and add these units to the sides of the unit from step 1.

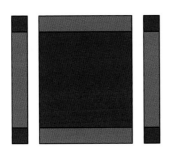

3. Add cream print 1½" x 8½" rectangles to the top and bottom of the unit from step 2. Add a navy 1½" square to each end of two cream print 1½" x 8½" rectangles and sew these units to the sides.

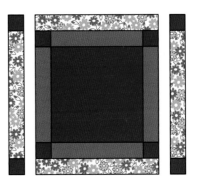

4. Sew red 1½" x 10½" rectangles to the top and bottom of the unit from step 3. Sew a navy 1½" square to each end of two red 1½" x 10½" rectangles and sew these units to the sides of the unit from step 3. Repeat the steps to make nine blocks.

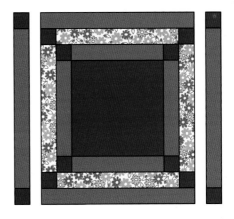

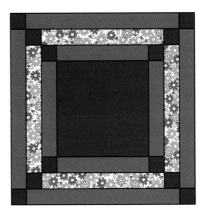

Make 9.

Quilted by Sue Urich • **Finished quilt:** 61½" x 61½" • **Finished block:** 12" x 12"

5. You should have 36 stars prepared for fusible appliqué. Appliqué four stars to the center square of each block, referring to the photo on page 38 for placement guidance. Refer to "Fusible Appliqué" on page 7 for more information as needed.

Quilt Assembly, Borders, and Finishing

1. Sew the blocks, setting squares, setting triangles, and corner triangles together in diagonal rows as shown. Sew the rows together. Trim and square up the sides and corners of the quilt as needed, leaving ¼" beyond the block corners for seam allowances.

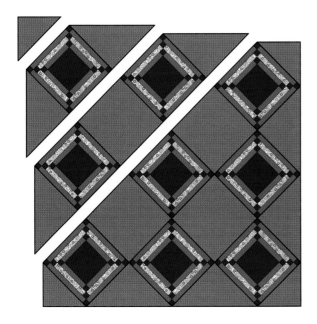

2. Stitch the six cream 1½"-wide inner-border strips together end to end. Refer to "Adding Borders" on page 8 to measure and cut the borders. Add the borders first to the top and bottom, and then to the sides.

3. Sew the six blue tone-on-tone 4½"-wide outer-border strips together end to end. Measure and cut the four border strips. Sew two of these strips to the top and bottom of the quilt. Sew a navy 4½" square to each end of the remaining two strips. Sew these units to the sides of the quilt.

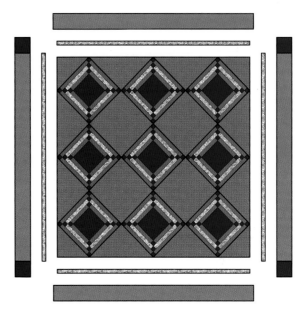

4. Layer the quilt top, batting, and backing. Quilt as desired.

5. Sew the blue tone-on-tone 1½"-wide binding strips together end to end. Stitch the binding to the quilt, referring to page 9 for more information.

Star
Cut 36.
Pattern is reversed for fusible appliqué.

Grandma's Sewing Basket Table Runner

The farmhouse I grew up in was the same house my grandma and grandpa lived in and my dad grew up in. It was a great old house that was chock-full of good memories. One of my favorite recollections is going through Grandma's sewing basket. It was full of treasures—thimbles, bits of rickrack, assorted buttons, scraps of wool left over from a crazy quilt, and balls of crochet thread.

On Sundays all of the aunts, uncles, and cousins would head to Grandma and Grandpa's for dinner. After dinner, we kids would look through Grandma's sewing basket for a thimble, and we'd play "Hide the Thimble" for hours. I was lucky enough to get to keep that sewing basket, complete with all of the goodies inside. This table runner uses some of those wonderful treasures as a tribute to Grandma and her sewing basket.

~Tammy

Materials

Yardage is based on 42"-wide fabric.

1¼ yards of green print for outer border and binding
½ yard of light blue checked fabric for background*
½ yard of cream striped fabric for basket appliqués
¼ yard of gold wool or cotton for flower appliqués
¼ yard of taupe plaid wool or cotton for flower-center appliqués
¼ yard of black print for inner border
⅛ yard of green wool or cotton for leaf appliqués
Scrap of taupe solid wool or cotton for seed appliqués (approximately 1½" x 18")
1⅝ yards of fabric for backing
24" x 54" piece of batting
2 yards of ⅜" wide ecru rickrack
6 assorted off-white buttons
1 yard of 18"-wide fusible web

If your fabric is not at least 41½" wide after removing selvages, you'll need 1¼ yards.

Cutting

The appliqué patterns are on page 44. For more information on cutting pieces for fusible appliqué, refer to "Fusible Appliqué" on page 7.

From the light blue checked fabric, cut:
1 rectangle, 11½" x 41½"

From the cream striped fabric, cut:
5 basket appliqués*

From the gold wool or cotton, cut:
5 flower-petals appliqués

From the taupe plaid wool or cotton, cut:
5 flower-center appliqués

From the green wool or cotton, cut:
10 leaf appliqués

Vary the position of the basket pattern on the stripes to add interest.

Finished table runner: 19" x 49"

From the taupe solid wool or cotton, cut:
15 seed appliqués

From the black print, cut:
2 strips, 1¼" x 41½"**
2 strips, 1¼" x 13"

From the green print, cut *on the lengthwise grain:*
2 strips, 3½" x 43"
2 strips, 3½" x 19"
4 binding strips, 1½" x 42"

***If your fabric is not wide enough, cut an extra strip
and piece together to get the needed length.*

Appliqué

Refer to "Fusible Appliqué" on page 7 and to
the photo on page 42 for placement guidance.
You should have five baskets prepared for fusible
appliqué.

1. Fold the 11½" x 41½" light blue checked background rectangle in half to find the center. Make
   a light crease and position one of the basket
   appliqués over the center crease, placing it
   approximately ½" from the raw edge.

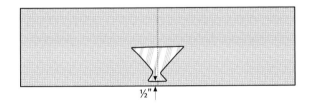

2. Position the remaining four baskets as shown.
   There should be approximately ⅜" between each
   basket. This is where the rickrack will be sewn.
   When you're happy with the basket placement,
   fuse in place.

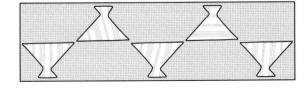

3. Position the flower petals and two leaves on each
   basket, tucking the ends of the leaves under the
   flowers. Note that I varied the placement of flowers slightly for each basket. Next, position the
   flower centers. Finally, position three flower-seed
   appliqués on each flower center. When you're
   happy with the placement, fuse in place. Stitch
   around the appliqué shapes with a machine blanket stitch and matching thread.

4. Position the rickrack, pinning it in place as
   you go. The rickrack curves should be approximately 4½" from the top edge of the baskets.
   Trim excess rickrack, and stitch in place with a
   machine straight stitch down the center of the
   rickrack.

Borders and Finishing

1. Sew the two 1¼" x 41½" black print strips to the
   top and bottom of the table runner. Sew the two
   1¼" x 13" black print strips to the sides.

2. Sew the two 3½" x 43" green print strips to the
   top and bottom of the table runner. Stitch the
   two 3½" x 19" green print strips to the sides.

3. Layer the quilt top, batting, and backing. Quilt
   as desired.

4. Sew the 1½"-wide green print binding strips
   together end to end. Stitch the binding to the
   quilt, referring to page 9 for help with binding.

5. Sew on the six buttons, one at each basket
   corner.

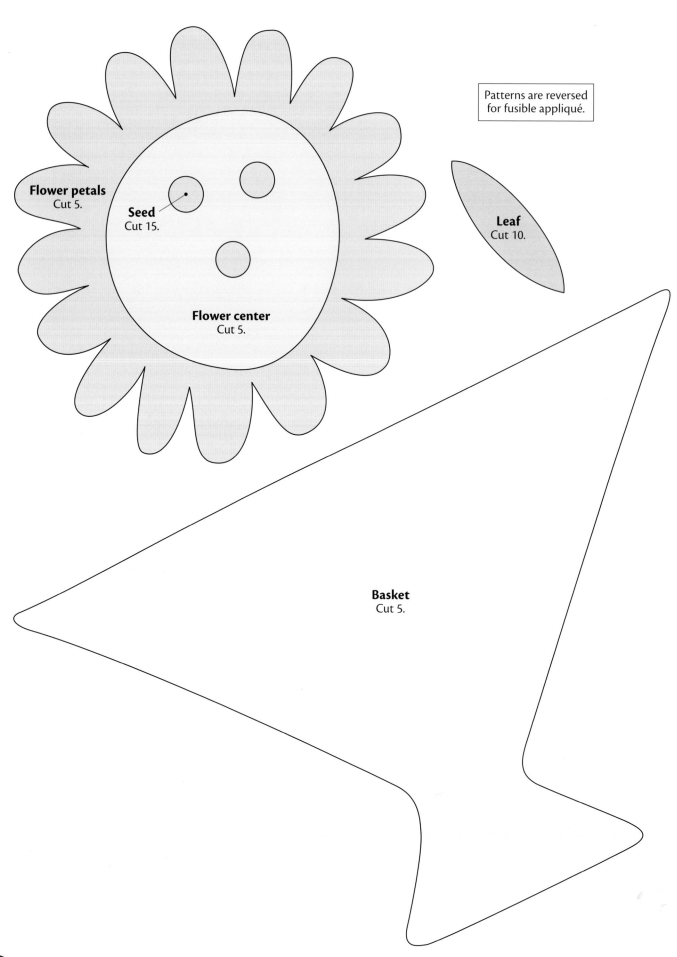

Patterns are reversed for fusible appliqué.

Flower petals
Cut 5.

Seed
Cut 15.

Leaf
Cut 10.

Flower center
Cut 5.

Basket
Cut 5.

Midnight Goldenrod

Every year about late August, you'll find goldenrod blooming in nearly every roadside ditch in Iowa. Goldenrod is a beautiful, stately, perennial wildflower. The plant grows to about four feet tall, and each spike is covered in brilliant gold flowers. The flowers are accented by wonderful sage green stem and leaves. They're plentiful and often found in large clumps.

One evening I was traveling down a country road and the car headlights shone on a patch of goldenrod. The stark contrast between the night sky and the brilliant gold of the flowers was very beautiful. This quilt is my version of goldenrod at night.

~Avis

Materials

Yardage is based on 42"-wide fabric.

2 yards of black fabric for Monkey Wrench blocks, pieced border, outer border, and binding

1⅔ yards of gold fabric for Monkey Wrench blocks, setting triangles, and pieced border

⅝ yard of dark orange print for Checkerboard blocks and inner border

⅜ yard of light print for Checkerboard blocks

¼ yard of light orange print for Checkerboard blocks

⅛ yard of yellow print for Checkerboard blocks

3 yards of fabric for backing

54" x 66" piece of batting

Cutting

Monkey Wrench Blocks

From the gold fabric, cut:

3 strips, 3¾" x 42", crosscut into 24 squares, 3¾" x 3¾". Cut each square in half diagonally to yield 48 triangles.

4 strips, 1⅞" x 42", crosscut into 44 rectangles, 1⅞" x 3⅜"

2 strips, 3⅜" x 42", crosscut into:
   12 squares, 3⅜" x 3⅜"
   4 rectangles, 1⅞" x 3⅜"

From the black fabric, cut:

3 strips, 3¾" x 42", crosscut into 24 squares, 3¾" x 3¾". Cut each square in half diagonally to yield 48 triangles.

5 strips, 2" x 42", crosscut into 48 rectangles, 2" x 3⅜"

Checkerboard Blocks

From the light print, cut:

1 strip, 2⅜" x 42", crosscut into 12 squares, 2⅜" x 2⅜"; cut each square in half diagonally to yield 24 corner triangles

2 strips, 4⅛" x 42", crosscut into 12 squares, 4⅛" x 4⅛"; cut each square into quarters diagonally to yield 48 side triangles

From the dark orange print, cut:

3 strips, 2½" x 42", crosscut into 48 squares, 2½" x 2½"

From the light orange print, cut:

2 strips, 2½" x 42", crosscut into 24 squares, 2½" x 2½"

From the yellow print, cut:

1 strip, 2½" x 42", crosscut into 6 squares, 2½" x 2½"

Setting Triangles, Borders, and Binding

From the gold fabric, cut:

3 squares, 15½" x 15½", cut each square into quarters diagonally to yield 12 triangles (2 are extra)

2 squares, 9" x 9", cut each square in half diagonally to yield 4 triangles

6 strips, 1½" x 42", crosscut into:

    32 rectangles, 1½" x 3"

    8 squares, 1½" x 1½"

    32 rectangles, 1½" x 3¾"

From the black fabric, cut:

6 strips, 1½" x 42", crosscut into:

    32 rectangles, 1½" x 3"

    8 squares, 1½" x 1½"

    32 rectangles, 1½" x 3¾"

6 strips, 2½" x 42"

6 binding strips, 1½" x 42"

From the dark orange print, cut:

5 strips, 1½" x 42"

Monkey Wrench Block Construction

1. Sew a gold triangle and a black triangle together. Make four units for each block.

Make 4.

2. Sew a gold 1⅞" x 3⅜" rectangle and a black 2" x 3⅜" rectangle together. Make four units for each block.

Make 4.

3. Sew the units from steps 1 and 2 and the gold 3⅜" square together as shown. Make 12 blocks. The blocks should measure 9⅛" x 9⅛".

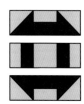

Make 12.

Checkerboard Block Construction

Sew eight dark orange print squares, four light orange print squares, one yellow print square, and the 12 light print triangles together in diagonal rows as shown. Make six blocks. The blocks should measure 9⅛" x 9⅛".

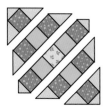

Make 6.

Quilt Assembly

1. Sew the blocks and triangles together in diagonal rows, following the diagram. The setting triangles were cut oversized and will be trimmed after assembly. Be sure to use an exact ¼" seam allowance when sewing the blocks together. Do *not* try to sew next to the corner points of the orange print squares in the Checkerboard blocks.

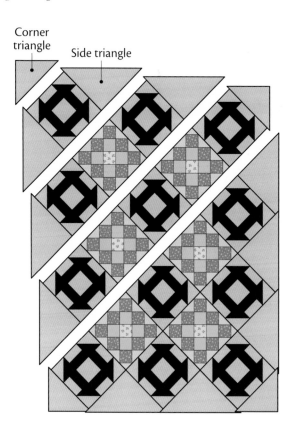

Corner triangle

Side triangle

Quilted by Sue Urich • **Finished quilt:** 48½" x 60½" • **Finished block:** 8⅝" x 8⅝"

2. Sew the rows together. Trim and square up the sides and corners of the quilt center so that it measures 38½" x 50½".

Borders and Finishing

1. For the inner border, stitch together three of the dark orange 1½"-wide strips, end to end. Then cut two 1½" x 50½" pieces and sew them to the sides of the quilt. Cut two 1½" x 40½" pieces from the remaining two strips and sew them to the top and bottom.

2. Sew a gold 1½" x 3" rectangle and a black 1½" x 3" rectangle together as shown. Make 32 units. Sew these units together as shown, in two rows of 16 units each. Sew these units to the top and bottom of the quilt.

Make 32.

Make 2.

3. In the same manner, sew a gold 1½" x 3¾" rectangle and a black 1½" x 3¾" rectangle together. Make 32 units. Sew these units together in two rows of 16 units each.

4. Sew two gold 1½" squares and two black 1½" squares together as shown to make a Four Patch block. Make four blocks.

Make 4.

5. Sew a Four Patch block to each end of the previously sewn rows as shown. Sew the pieced strips to the sides of the quilt.

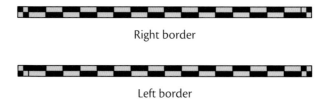

Right border

Left border

6. For the outer border, sew the black 2½"-wide strips together end to end, and then cut two 2½" x 56" strips and sew them to the sides of the quilt. Cut two 2½" x 48½" strips and stitch them to the top and bottom.

7. Layer the quilt top, batting, and backing. Quilt as desired.

8. Sew the black 1½"-wide binding strips together end to end. Sew the binding to the quilt, referring to page 9 for more information on binding.

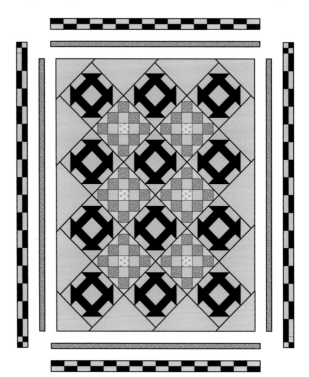

Tulip Fields

In Iowa, our farms are a sea of green from May through August. In September the crops start maturing and we get a colorful show. The beans slowly turn from green, to a brilliant gold, and finally to a deep rust. The corn stalks dry and turn a pale gold. It's a lovely sight.

One spring, I was lucky enough to visit the tulip farms in the state of Washington with my family. Now that was a colorful sight! The fields were full of tulips in full bloom in every color imaginable. My favorites were the red and pink tulip fields. Sometimes I wish we could have beautiful tulip fields in Iowa. I don't think that will happen anytime soon, so I have stitched up this quilt to remind me of that beautiful sight and the wonderful memories we made on that spring trip to Washington.

~Tammy

Materials

Yardage is based on 42"-wide fabric.

1½ yards of taupe plaid for sashing, outer border, and binding

1 yard of light pink print for appliqué block background and pieced blocks

⅝ yard of medium pink print for pieced blocks and tulip-accent appliqués

⅝ yard of light print for pieced blocks

½ yard of green print for pieced blocks and leaf and stem appliqués

½ yard of red print for tulip and circle appliqués, sashing squares, and border corner squares

⅜ yard of ecru print for sashing and inner border

⅓ yard of red solid for pieced blocks

2⅝ yards of fabric for backing

45" x 68" piece of batting

2 yards of 18"-wide fusible web

Cutting

The appliqué patterns are on page 55. For more information on cutting pieces for fusible appliqué, refer to "Fusible Appliqué" on page 7.

From the light print, cut:

2 strips, 3⅞" x 42", crosscut into 16 squares, 3⅞" x 3⅞"; cut each square in half diagonally to yield 32 triangles

4 strips, 2" x 42", crosscut into 64 squares, 2" x 2"

From the medium pink print, cut:

2 strips, 3⅞" x 42", crosscut into 16 squares, 3⅞" x 3⅞"; cut each square in half diagonally to yield 32 triangles

1 strip, 3½" x 42", crosscut into 8 squares, 3½" x 3½"

28 of each of the tulip accent shapes

From the light pink print, cut:

3 strips, 3½" x 42", crosscut into 32 squares, 3½" x 3½"

2 strips, 9½" x 42", crosscut into 7 squares, 9½" x 9½"

From the red solid, cut:

4 strips, 2" x 42", crosscut into 64 squares, 2" x 2"

From the green print, cut:

2 strips, 2" x 42", crosscut into 32 squares, 2" x 2"

28 leaf appliqués

14 stem appliqués

From the red print, cut:

4 squares, 3½" x 3½"

8 squares, 3" x 3"

28 tulip appliqués

7 circle appliqués

From the ecru print, cut:

11 strips, 1" x 42", crosscut 8 of the strips into:

    22 rectangles, 1" x 9½"

    2 strips, 1" x 32½"

From the taupe plaid, cut:

11 strips, 1½" x 42", crosscut into 44 rectangles,

    1½" x 9½"

5 strips, 3½" x 42", cut 2 of these into 2 strips,

    3½" x 33½"

6 binding strips, 1½" x 42"

Pieced Block Construction

1. Stitch together a light background triangle and a medium pink triangle. Make 32 units.

Make 32.

2. Refer to "Folded Corners" on page 6 to mark and lay a light background 2" square on the upper-left corner of a light pink 3½" square. Stitch along the diagonal line, trim, and press as shown.

3. Lay a second light background 2" square on the upper-right corner of the light pink square. Stitch along the diagonal, trim, and press.

4. Repeat this process with two red solid 2" squares on the lower two corners of the pink square. Repeat to make a total of 32 units.

Make 32.

5. Using the folded-corners technique, sew four green 2" squares to a medium pink 3½" square. Make eight units.

Make 8.

6. Sew the units together in rows as shown, and then join the rows. Make eight blocks.

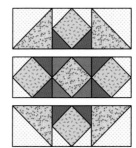 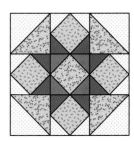

Make 8.

Quilted by Sue Urich • **Finished quilt:** 39½" x 62½" • **Finished block:** 9" x 9"

Tulip Block Appliqué

Refer to "Fusible Appliqué" on page 7 and to the photo on page 53 for placement guidance. You'll need four tulips, four leaf units, two stems, one circle, and four of each of the tulip accent shapes for each block.

1. Fold the light pink 9½" square diagonally and press lightly. Open it out and fold the square diagonally in the opposite direction and press lightly. This will give you a guideline for stem placement.

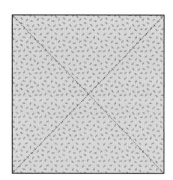

2. Position the stems on the pressed lines. Then, carefully tuck the leaf unit under the stems, approximately ½" from the end of the stems. Position the tulips, covering the ends of the stems. Position three tulip accent shapes on each tulip. Finally, position the circle in the center of the block. When you're happy with the placement, fuse in place.

3. Stitch around the appliqués using a machine blanket stitch and matching thread. Make a total of seven blocks.

Make 7.

Quilt Assembly

1. Sew a taupe plaid 1½" x 9½" rectangle to each side of an ecru print 1" x 9½" rectangle. Make 22 sashing units.

Make 22.

2. Sew two sashing units and three blocks together in rows as shown.

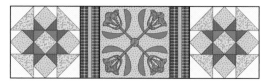

Make 3.

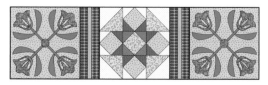

Make 2.

3. Sew three sashing units and two red 3" sashing squares together as shown. Make four rows.

Make 4.

4. Sew the block rows and sashing rows together as shown.

Borders and Finishing

Before cutting and adding borders, measure your quilt through the center, referring to "Adding Borders" on page 8. Cut the borders to your specific lengths if the measurements are different from those given below.

1. Sew the two ecru 1" x 32½" strips for the inner border to the top and bottom of the quilt.

2. Sew the three ecru 1" x 42" strips together end to end. Cut two 56½" strips and sew them to the sides of the quilt.

3. Sew the taupe plaid 3½" x 33½" strips for the outer border to the top and bottom of the quilt.

4. Sew the remaining three taupe plaid 3½" x 42" strips together end to end. Cut two 56½"-long strips and sew a red print 3½" square to each end of these strips. Sew the strips to the sides of the quilt.

5. Layer the quilt top, batting, and backing. Quilt as desired.

6. Sew the taupe plaid 1½"-wide binding strips together end to end and sew the binding to the quilt. Refer to page 9 for binding information.

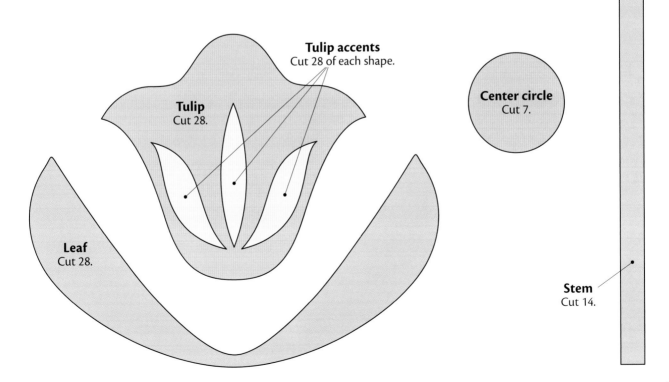

Tulip accents
Cut 28 of each shape.

Tulip
Cut 28.

Center circle
Cut 7.

Leaf
Cut 28.

Stem
Cut 14.

Snow on Furrowed Ground

*E*very fall, after the crops have been harvested, the ground is turned under with a plow. The black slabs of earth sit silently all winter, often covered with a thick blanket of snow. Rain, sleet, and snow fall on the fields, breaking down the furrowed ground. In the spring, the ground has turned into a rich, loamy soil, just perfect to start the growing season all over again. The colors in this quilt remind me of freshly fallen snow covering the furrowed ground. The touch of red symbolizes the beautiful red barns that dot the countryside.

~Avis

Materials

Yardage is based on 42"-wide fabric.

¼ yard *each* of 12 assorted black prints for blocks

⅔ yard *each* of 4 assorted light prints for blocks

2 yards of black solid or black tone-on-tone fabric for outer border and binding

1¼ yards of gray print for sashing and inner border

⅛ yard of red print for sashing squares

5 yards of fabric for backing

71" x 88" piece of batting

Cutting

From *each* of the 12 assorted black prints, cut:

1 strip, 3⅞" x 42", crosscut into 6 squares, 3⅞" x 3⅞"; cut each square in half diagonally to yield 12 triangles

2 strips, 1½" x 42", crosscut into:
    16 squares, 1½" x 1½"
    8 rectangles, 1½" x 3½"

From *each* of the 4 assorted light prints, cut:

2 strips, 3⅞" x 42", crosscut into 18 squares, 3⅞" x 3⅞"; cut each square in half diagonally to yield 36 triangles

2 strips, 3½" x 42", crosscut into 15 squares, 3½" x 3½"

4 strips, 1½" x 42", crosscut into:
    60 squares, 1½" x 1½"
    12 rectangles, 1½" x 3½"

From the gray print, cut:

9 strips, 2½" x 42", crosscut into 17 rectangles, 2½" x 15½"

6 strips, 2½" x 42"

From the red print, cut:

6 squares, 2½" x 2½"

From the black tone-on-tone fabric, cut:

7 strips, 6" x 42"

8 binding strips, 1½" x 42"

Block Construction

The instructions are written for making one block at a time. You'll make one block using each black print and three blocks using each light print.

1. Sew 12 black 3⅞" triangles to 12 light 3⅞" triangles to make 12 half-square-triangle units.

Make 12.

2. Stitch together four black 1½" squares and five light 1½" squares as shown to make a nine-patch unit. Make four.

Make 4.

3. Sew two black rectangles and one light rectangle together as shown. Make four.

Make 4.

4. Sew the units from steps 1–3 together in rows, adding five light 3½" squares as shown.

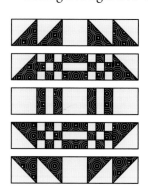 

5. Repeat steps 1–4 to make 12 blocks.

Quilt Assembly

1. Sew three blocks and two gray 2½" x 15½" sashing strips together as shown. Make four rows.

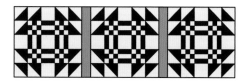

Make 4.

2. Sew three sashing strips and two red 2½" squares together as shown. Make three rows.

Make 3.

3. Sew the block and sashing rows together, as shown.

Borders and Finishing

It's always a good idea to measure the length and width of your quilt through the center before cutting borders. See "Adding Borders" on page 8. If your dimensions vary from those given, cut the borders to match your quilt.

1. For the inner border, stitch the six gray 2½" x 42" strips together end to end. Cut two 2½" x 49½" strips and sew them to the top and bottom of the quilt. Then cut two 2½" x 70½" strips and stitch them to the sides.

2. For the outer border, sew the black 6"-wide strips together end to end. Cut two 6" x 53½" strips and sew them to the top and bottom of the quilt. Cut two 6" x 81½" strips and stitch them to the sides of the quilt.

3. Layer the quilt top, batting, and backing. Quilt as desired.

4. Sew the black 1½"-wide binding strips together end to end. Sew the binding to the quilt, referring to page 9 for binding help if needed.

Quilted by Sue Urich • **Finished quilt:** 64½" x 81½" • **Finished block:** 15" x 15"

The Scrap Yard

This bright and colorful quilt is a great example of true farm life! You may wonder why; let me explain. The pieced blocks, you'll notice, are red, blue, green, and brown. Those colors represent the tractors that are parked in the grove for "spare parts." Red is for Case IH, blue is for Ford, green is for John Deere, and the brown . . . well, that's for the tractors and other spare farm equipment that has become so rusty that all of the paint is gone. The grove is the perfect place to park this rolling fleet of spare parts. Some pieces of equipment are actually used for parts, but others sit so long in the grove that wildflowers and native grasses eventually grow up and around the equipment.

A farmer has much in common with a quilter; each has patience and believes that a little hard work will make a good crop, or that a little stitching will turn that stash of fabric into a great quilt. The spare parts in the grove are a farmer's scrap yard and are just like the cupboards or shelves that hold our fabric. This quilt is a tribute to all hard-working farmers and their scrap yards.

~Avis

Materials

Yardage is based on 42"-wide fabric.

1 yard of light fabric for appliquéd block backgrounds, setting triangles, and corner triangles

1 yard of brown print for outer border and binding

¼ yard *each of 4 assorted light prints* for pieced blocks

½ yard of red print for pieced blocks and flower appliqués

½ yard of blue print for pieced blocks and flower appliqués

½ yard of dark pink tone-on-tone print for flower appliqués and inner border

¼ yard of dark green print for pieced blocks

¼ yard of brown print for pieced blocks

¼ yard of yellow fabric for flower appliqués

¼ yard of medium green print for circle, half circle, and quarter circle appliqués

¼ yard of light green fabric for leaf appliqués

3 yards of fabric for backing

52" x 52" square of batting

2 yards of 18"-wide fusible web

Cutting

The appliqué patterns are on page 65. For more information on cutting pieces for fusible appliqué, refer to "Fusible Appliqué" on page 7.

From *each* of the 4 assorted light prints, cut:

5 squares, 5¾" x 5¾", cut each square into quarters diagonally to yield 20 triangles (2 are extra)

From *each* of the blue, brown, dark green, and red prints, cut:

5 squares, 5¾" x 5¾", cut each square into quarters diagonally to yield 20 triangles (2 are extra)

From the light fabric, cut:

2 squares, 13⅞" x 13⅞", cut each square into quarters diagonally to yield 8 triangles

4 squares, 9½" x 9½"

2 squares, 7¼" x 7¼", cut each square in half diagonally to yield 4 triangles

From the blue print, cut:

18 flower appliqués

From the red print, cut:
18 flower appliqués

From the yellow fabric, cut:
18 flower appliqués

From the dark pink tone-on-tone print, cut:
4 strips, 1½" x 42"
18 flower appliqués

From the medium green print, cut:
4 circle appliqués
8 half-circle appliqués
4 quarter-circle appliqués

From the light green fabric, cut:
72 leaf appliqués

From the brown print for outer border and binding, cut:
5 strips, 3½" x 42"
5 binding strips, 1½" x 42"

Block Construction

1. Pair 18 light print 5¾" triangles with 18 blue triangles. Sew them together along the short sides as shown. Make 18 units. Repeat for the brown, green, and red triangles, pairing each with a different light print.

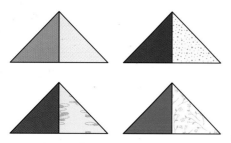

Make 18 of each color combination.

2. Sew the units from step 1 together to make nine blocks of each color combination.

3. Sew four blocks together (one from each color combination) to complete the larger block. Make nine blocks.

Make 9.

Floral Block Appliqué

Refer to "Fusible Appliqué" on page 7 and to the photo on page 63 for placement guidance. Be sure to position all of the appliqué shapes before fusing to allow for placement adjustment.

1. Fold the light 9½" background squares diagonally and press a light crease. Fold again in the opposite direction and make another crease to use as a placement guide.

2. Place a green circle in the center of a light square. Then position eight flowers, two from each color, and eight leaves. When you're happy with the placement, fuse in place. Make four blocks.

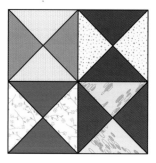

Make 4.

Quilted by Sue Urich • **Finished quilt:** 46¾" x 46¾" • **Finished block:** 9" x 9"

3. Appliqué the setting triangles, placing the half-circle shape in the middle of the long side of the triangle. The straight edge of the half circle will be even with the edge of the triangle. Position four flowers and four leaves as shown; fuse in place.

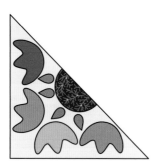

Make 8.

4. Appliqué the corner triangles, placing the quarter-circle shape in the 90° corner of the triangle. Position two flowers and two leaves as shown; fuse in place.

Make 2.

Make 2.

5. After fusing the shapes in place, stitch around them with a machine blanket stitch and matching thread. Handle the triangles carefully to avoid stretching the bias edges.

Quilt Assembly

Stitch the pieced blocks, appliquéd blocks, setting triangles, and corner triangles together in diagonal rows as shown.

Borders and Finishing

1. Refer to "Adding Borders" on page 8 to measure and add the dark pink tone-on-tone 1½"-wide inner-border strips to the sides of the quilt. Measure and add the inner borders to the top and bottom, piecing strips if necessary.

2. Join the brown print 3½"-wide strips end to end to make one long strip. Measure, cut, and add the outer borders as you did the inner borders.

3. Layer the quilt top, batting, and backing. Quilt as desired.

4. Sew the brown print 1½"-wide binding strips together end to end. Sew the binding to the quilt, referring to page 9 for more help with binding.

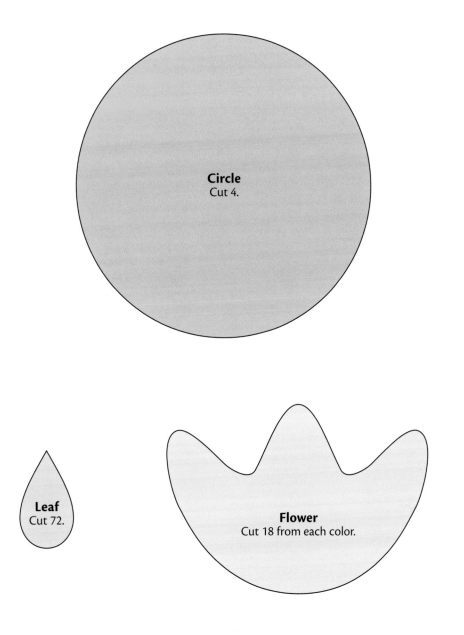

Circle
Cut 4.

Leaf
Cut 72.

Flower
Cut 18 from each color.

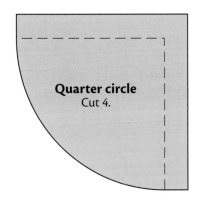

Quarter circle
Cut 4.

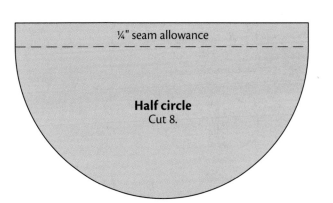

¼" seam allowance

Half circle
Cut 8.

Country Roads

In Iowa, the countryside is divided into square-mile sections, for the most part. These sections are outlined by either gravel or paved roads. The gravel roads are narrower than the paved roads, and they do not have any center-line markings. When you're driving on a gravel road and meet an oncoming car, both cars move over to the sides of the road, give a friendly wave, and then continue down the road.

I lived on a farm that was surrounded by gravel roads. Many times our family would go for bike rides around the section. There would always be red-winged blackbirds, singing constantly as they sat on the fence posts or on the power lines. I think those birds are lovely—as long as they're just sitting there. During nesting time, however, the male birds become very protective of their territory. They would swoop down at us as we were riding our bikes to drive us away from their nests. Now, I'm not good with birds swooping down at me—maybe I watched the movie *The Birds* one too many times. I would peddle my bike as fast as my legs could go to get away from those darn birds.

This quilt represents those country roads—the paved roads with the center line marked and the narrower gravel roads—and those red-winged blackbirds that you see in abundance, no matter what road you're on.

~Tammy

Materials

Yardage is based on 42"-wide fabric.

1⅝ yards of black solid for rounds 1–5 and binding

⅞ yard of brown plaid for outer border

¾ yard of cream print for round 4

½ yard of dark tan print for round 2

⅜ yard of tan plaid for round 3

⅜ yard of red print 4 for round 4

⅜ yard of red print 5 for round 5

⅓ yard of red print 3 for round 3

¼ yard of brown print for center rectangle

¼ yard of tan checked fabric for round 1

¼ yard of red print 1 for round 1

¼ yard of red print 2 for round 2

3⅓ yards of fabric for backing

60" x 68" piece of batting

8½ yards of ¾"-wide black rickrack

Cutting

From the brown print, cut:

1 rectangle, 6½" x 10½"

Round 1

From the black solid, cut:

4 squares, 3¼" x 3¼", cut each square into quarters diagonally to yield 16 triangles

From red print 1, cut:

3 squares, 3¼" x 3¼", cut each square into quarters diagonally to yield 12 triangles

4 squares, 1⅞" x 1⅞", cut each square in half diagonally to yield 8 triangles

4 squares, 1½" x 1½"

From the tan checked fabric, cut:

2 rectangles, 2½" x 8½"

2 rectangles, 2½" x 16½"

Round 2

From the black solid, cut:

4 squares, 5¼" x 5¼", cut each square into quarters
diagonally to yield 16 triangles (2 are extra)

From red print 2, cut:

3 squares, 5¼" x 5¼", cut each square into quarters
diagonally to yield 12 triangles (2 are extra)
4 squares, 2⅞" x 2⅞", cut each square in half
diagonally to yield 8 triangles
4 squares, 2½" x 2½"

From the dark tan print, cut:

2 rectangles, 4½" x 16½"
2 rectangles, 4½" x 28½"

Round 3

From the black solid, cut:

7 squares, 5¼" x 5¼", cut each square into quarters
diagonally to yield 28 triangles (2 are extra)

From red print 3, cut:

6 squares, 5¼" x 5¼", cut each square into quarters
diagonally to yield 24 triangles (2 are extra)
4 squares, 2⅞" x 2⅞", cut each square in half
diagonally to yield 8 triangles
4 squares, 2½" x 2½"

From the tan plaid, cut:

2 strips, 2½" x 28½"
2 strips, 2½" x 36½"

Round 4

From the black solid, cut:

9 squares, 5¼" x 5¼", cut each square into quarters
diagonally to yield 36 triangles (2 are extra)

From red print 4, cut:

8 squares, 5¼" x 5¼", cut each square into quarters
diagonally to yield 32 triangles (2 are extra)
4 squares, 2⅞" x 2⅞", cut each square in half
diagonally to yield 8 triangles
4 squares, 2½" x 2½"

From the cream print, cut:

2 strips, 4½" x 36½"
3 strips, 4½" x 42"

Round 5

From the black solid, cut:

12 squares, 5¼" x 5¼", cut each square into quarters
diagonally to yield 48 triangles (2 are extra)

From red print 5, cut:

11 squares, 5¼" x 5¼", cut each square into quarters
diagonally to yield 44 triangles (2 are extra)
4 squares, 2⅞" x 2⅞", cut each square in half
diagonally to yield 8 triangles
4 squares, 2½" x 2½"

Outer Border and Binding

From the brown plaid, cut:

3 strips, 5½" x 42"
3 strips, 3½" x 42"

From the black solid, cut:

6 strips, 1½" x 42"

Round 1

1. Sew three black and two red print 1 quarter-
square triangles together along the short sides,
offsetting the points by ¼". Add a smaller red
half-square triangle to each end. Make two rows.

Make 2.

2. Sew the rows to the top and bottom of the brown
print rectangle.

Quilted by Sue Urich • **Finished quilt:** 54½" x 62½"

3. Sew five black and four red print 1 quarter-square triangles together in a row. Add a smaller red triangle to each end as before. Then add two red 1½" squares to each end. Make two rows and sew them to the sides of the rectangle.

4. Sew tan checked 2½" x 8½" rectangles to the top and bottom of the unit. Sew tan checked 2½" x 16½" rectangles to the sides.

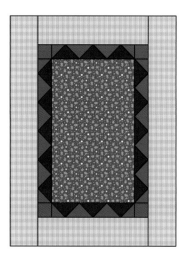

Round 2

1. In the same manner as before, stitch three black and two red print 2 quarter-square triangles together. Add a small red triangle to each end. Make two rows. Sew the rows to the top and bottom of the unit from round 1. Sew four black and three red large triangles together. Add a small red

triangle and a red 2½" square to each end. Make two rows and sew them to the sides.

2. Sew the two dark tan print 4½" x 16½" rectangles to the top and bottom of the unit. Sew the dark tan print 4½" x 28½" rectangles to the sides.

3. Cut two pieces of rickrack an inch or so longer than the side strips. Lay the rickrack down the center of the side strips and stitch down the center with matching thread. In the same manner, lay the rickrack on the top and bottom strips and sew down the center. When centering the rickrack, be sure to allow for the ¼" seam allowance along the raw edge.

Round 3

1. Sew six black and five red print 3 quarter-square triangles together and add two small red triangles as before. Make two rows. Add these rows to the top and bottom of the unit from round 2. Then sew seven black and six red print 3 triangles together, adding the small red triangles and two red squares to the ends. Make two rows. Sew the rows to the sides.

2. Sew the tan plaid 2½" x 28½" strips to the top and bottom. Then sew the 2½" x 36½" strips to the sides.

Round 4

1. Sew eight black and seven red print 4 quarter-square triangles together; add a small red triangle to each end. Make two rows. Sew the rows to the top and bottom of the unit from round 3. Sew together nine black and eight red triangles. Add the small triangles to the ends, and then add the two red squares. Make two rows and stitch them to the sides of the quilt.

2. Sew the cream print 4½" x 36½" strips to the top and bottom. Sew the three cream print 4½" x 42" strips together end to end, and then cut two strips, 4½" x 48½". Sew these to the

sides. Apply the rickrack to these pieces as before.

Round 5

1. Sew 11 black and 10 red print 5 quarter-square triangles together; add the two smaller red triangles. Make two rows and sew them to the top and bottom of the quilt.

2. Sew together 12 black triangles, 11 red print 5 triangles, two small red triangles, and two red squares. Make two rows. Sew the rows to the sides of the quilt.

Outer Border and Finishing

It's always a good idea to measure the length and width of your quilt through the center before cutting borders. See "Adding Borders" on page 8. If your dimensions vary from those given, cut the borders to match your quilt.

1. Sew the three brown plaid 5½" x 42" strips together end to end. Cut two 48½"-long strips. Sew these to the top and bottom of the quilt.

2. Sew the three brown plaid 3½" x 42" strips together end to end. Cut two 62½"-long strips. Stitch these strips to the sides of the quilt.

3. Layer the quilt top, batting, and backing. Quilt as desired.

4. Sew the black 1½"-wide binding strips together end to end. Sew the binding to the quilt. Refer to page 9 for more help with binding.

Sunrise in the Farm Garden

In addition to being grain farmers, my parents raised cattle and had milk cows, chickens, and pigs. There were livestock chores every morning and night: cows to be milked and put out to pasture, cattle and pigs to be fed, eggs to be gathered, and chickens to be fed. Mother helped Dad with all of the grain farming and the livestock chores. Yet somehow she found time to plant and tend a large vegetable garden. The garden was big enough that

she canned or froze enough food to feed our family of four for the entire year. She also grew apples, raspberries, and strawberries that she made into pies or jams.

Mother also found time to maintain stunning flower-beds. These flowerbeds were such a thing of beauty— vivid shades of orange, red, and yellow everywhere. This quilt is dedicated to my mom. She loved sunrises, flowers, and most of all she loved living on the farm. Thanks, Mom—I learned so much from you!

~Avis

Materials

Yardage is based on 42"-wide fabric.

2⅛ yards of peach fabric for flower appliqués, outer border, and binding

1¼ yards of light fabric for appliquéd block backgrounds

1⅛ yards of rose polka-dot fabric for outer border

1⅛ yards of brown print for pieced blocks

½ yard of green fabric for pieced blocks

⅜ yard of light green fabric for leaf appliqués

⅓ yard of rose solid for flower appliqués

⅓ yard of dark green print for stem appliqués

⅓ yard of pink striped fabric for inner border

4 yards of fabric for backing

69" x 69" square of batting

2 yards of 18"-wide fusible web

Cutting

The appliqué patterns are on page 78. For more information on cutting pieces for fusible appliqué, refer to "Fusible Appliqué" on page 7.

From the brown print, cut:

20 strips, 1⅝" x 42", crosscut into:
    48 rectangles, 1⅝" x 7¼"
    48 rectangles, 1⅝" x 5"
    48 rectangles, 1⅝" x 2¾"

From the green fabric for pieced blocks, cut:

6 strips, 1⅝" x 42", crosscut into 144 squares, 1⅝" x 1⅝"

1 strip, 2¾" x 42", crosscut into 12 squares, 2¾" x 2¾"

From the light fabric, cut:

4 strips, 9½" x 42", crosscut into 13 squares, 9½" x 9½"

From the rose polka-dot fabric, cut:

1 strip, 8⅞" x 42", crosscut into 4 squares, 8⅞" x 8⅞";
cut each square in half diagonally to yield
8 triangles

3 strips, 8½" x 42"

From the rose solid, cut:

13 large flower-base appliqués
26 small flower-base appliqués

From the dark green print, cut:

13 center stem appliqués
13 stem 1 appliqués
13 stem 2 appliqués

From the light green fabric, cut:

13 large leaf 1 appliqués
13 large leaf 2 appliqués
13 small leaf 1 appliqués
13 small leaf 2 appliqués

From the peach fabric, cut:

5 strips, 8½" x 42", crosscut *1 strip* into 4 squares,
8½" x 8½"

7 binding strips, 1½" x 42"

13 large flower appliqués

26 small flower appliqués

From the pink striped fabric, cut:

5 strips, 1½" x 42"

Pieced Block Construction

1. Sew brown 1⅝" x 2¾" rectangles to opposite
   sides of a green 2¾" square. Sew a green 1⅝"
   square to each end of two brown 1⅝" x 2¾"
   rectangles. Sew the units together as shown.

2. Sew a brown 1⅝" x 5" rectangle to each side of
   the unit from step 1. Sew a green 1⅝" square to
   each end of two brown 1⅝" x 5" rectangles. Sew
   them to the top and bottom of the unit as shown.

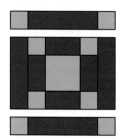

3. Sew brown 1⅝" x 7¼" rectangles to the sides of
   the block. Sew two green 1⅝" squares to each
   end of two brown 1⅝" x 7¼" rectangles. Sew
   these units to the top and bottom of the block.

4. Repeat steps 1–3 to make 12 blocks.

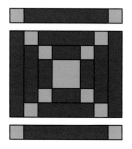

Make 12.

Floral Block Appliqué

Refer to "Fusible Appliqué" on page 7 and to the
photo on page 75 for placement guidance. Position
all of the appliqué shapes before fusing in place to
allow for placement adjustment.

1. Fold a light 9½" background square in half and
   make a vertical crease. Position the center stem
   on the crease, ensuring the bottom end of the
   stem is even with the bottom edge of the block.
   Position the right stem about 3" up from the
   bottom and the left stem about 4" up from the
   bottom, tucking the ends under the center stem.

2. Position two large leaves below the right and left
   stems and two small leaves above those stems.

Quilted by Sue Urich • **Finished quilt:** 63" x 63" • **Finished block:** 9" x 9"

3. Position the large flower and two small flowers next. Finally, position the large flower base and two small flower bases. When you're happy with the placement, fuse in place.

4. Stitch around the appliqués with a machine blanket stitch and matching thread. Make 13 appliquéd blocks.

Make 13.

Quilt Assembly

1. Sew the blocks together in five rows of five blocks each as shown.

Make 3.

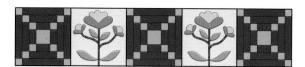

Make 2.

2. Sew the rows together, alternating them.

Borders and Finishing

1. Sew the five pink striped 1½" x 42" strips together end to end for the inner border. Cut two 45½"-long strips and sew them to the sides of the quilt. Then cut two 47½"-long strips and stitch them to the top and bottom of the quilt.

2. For the outer border, you'll cut large triangles from the rose solid 8½" x 42" strips and the peach 8½" x 42" strips. Begin by making a pencil mark at the beginning of a rose solid strip; make another mark 16⅞"from the first mark. On the opposite side of the strip, mark the halfway point of 16⅞". You can do this by folding the strip to find the center or by making a pencil mark at a point between 8⅜" and 8½" (8⁷⁄₁₆").

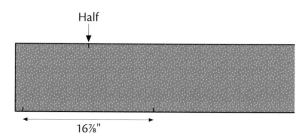

Half

16⅞"

3. Draw a line at a 45° angle from the center point to the two pencil marks as shown. Cut the triangle out on the drawn lines. Use the triangle to make a template from card stock or template plastic. Cut eight triangles from the rose strips and twelve from the peach strips.

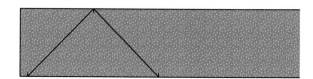

4. Sew three peach triangles and two rose solid triangles together along the short sides as shown, offsetting the points by ¼". Sew a smaller rose solid triangle to each end. Make four border strips.

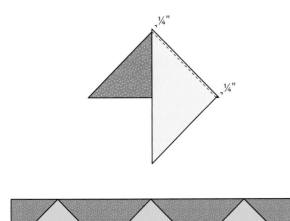

Make 4.

5. Sew two of the border strips to the top and bottom of the quilt. Sew a peach 8½" square to each end of the remaining two strips. Sew these to the sides.

6. Layer the quilt top, batting, and backing. Quilt as desired.

7. Sew the peach 1½"-wide binding strips together end to end. Sew the binding to the quilt. For more help with binding, refer to page 9.

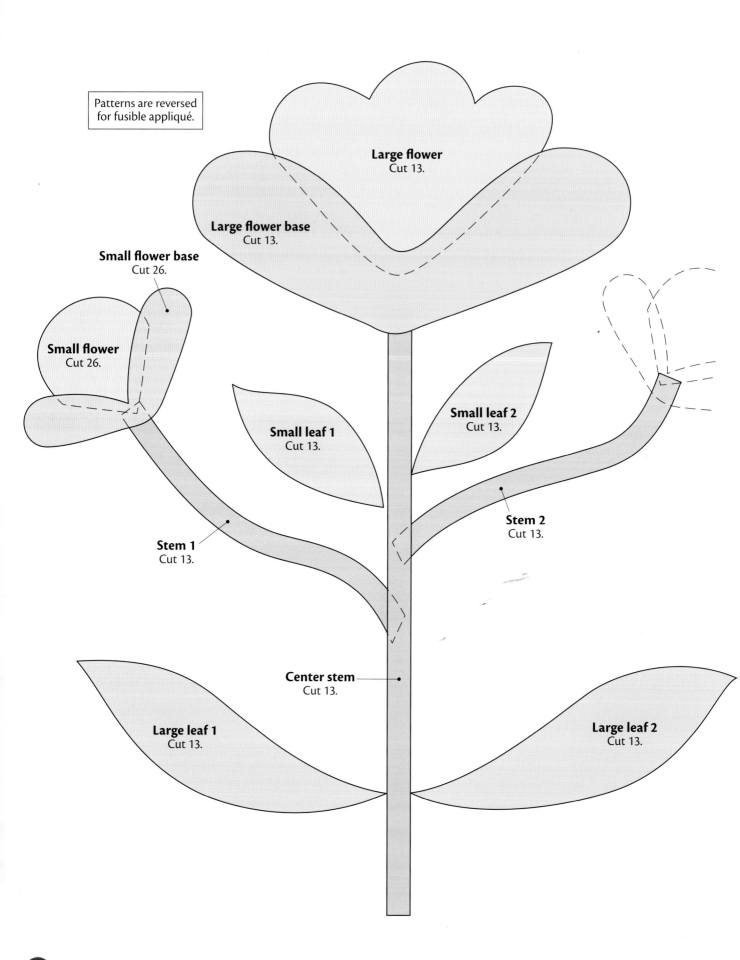

Patterns are reversed
for fusible appliqué.

Large flower
Cut 13.

Large flower base
Cut 13.

Small flower base
Cut 26.

Small flower
Cut 26.

Small leaf 1
Cut 13.

Small leaf 2
Cut 13.

Stem 1
Cut 13.

Stem 2
Cut 13.

Center stem
Cut 13.

Large leaf 1
Cut 13.

Large leaf 2
Cut 13.

About the Authors

Avis Shirer and Tammy Johnson and have published 12 quilt books, including *Folk-Art Favorites* (Martingale & Company, 2009), and more than 200 patterns, including their popular Hanging on a Star series and the Button Up series. They've also designed several lines of fabric. They're well known for their primitive, whimsical designs, and they love to combine many elements in their quilt designs, including appliqué, patchwork, and traditional quilting fabrics as well as wool, rickrack, buttons, and more to add to the overall charm.

There's More Online!

- For more information about Avis and Tammy's books and patterns, visit www.joinedatthehip.com.

- To find other great books on quilting, knitting, crochet, and more, visit www.martingale-pub.com.

You might also enjoy these other fine titles from

Martingale & Company

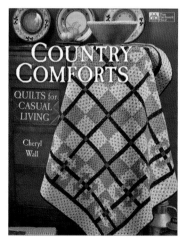

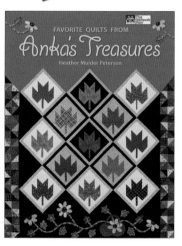

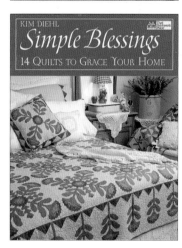

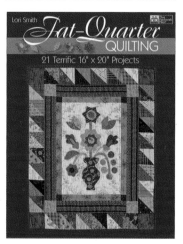

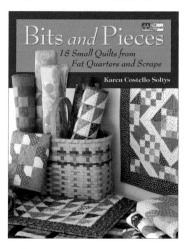

Our books are available at bookstores and your favorite craft, fabric, and yarn retailers.
Visit us at www.martingale-pub.com or contact us at:

Martingale®
& C O M P A N Y

1-800-426-3126
International: 1-425-483-3313
Fax: 1-425-486-7596
Email: info@martingale-pub.com

America's Best-Loved Quilt Books® America's Best-Loved Craft & Hobby Books®
America's Best-Loved Knitting Books®